Today is A Great Day To Manifest The S#*t Out Of Some Abundance

A Guide to The Exciting New Era of
Human Capability and Potential

Bill Newell

This book is dedicated to you!

Yes, You!

CONTENTS

INTRODUCTION

"The magic we experience in our youth ought not be
sacrificed in the name of societal obligations."
-Bill Newell

The early years of our existence as human beings are
brimming with phenomenal sensory vitality. Effervescent
chemical reactions surge through immaculate corridors in
our physical bodies, igniting eruptions throughout our
celestial faculties. The synergy between these divine realms
within us is not only exhilarating but defining. From these
events we discern the perceptions of reality that tend to
guide us through our entire lives. The perception of events
has the ability to alter your physical DNA. Information
acquired through the senses is encoded into the very fabric
of your being and governs your existence before it is
passed down to future generations.

You did not come across this book by accident. This
occurrence has a definitive purpose in your life, as do all
the occurrences you will ever experience. The beautiful
fact of the matter is that you chose this experience
consciously and subconsciously and only you can decide
what the purpose of it is as well. You have chosen this
experience because you are searching for a way to live a
more exuberant life. You wish to embody as much of your
unlimited potential as possible and you're wondering how.
You feel as though you are wandering through life doing
your best to avoid pitfalls and malevolent forces and you
want to strengthen your arsenal against all the nitty gritty
details of life as we know it. Well guess what, you have just
entered a new realm, that you have never known before.
The information contained herein will change you and the
entire world that you perceive from the molecular level all
the way up to the macrocosm and beyond. Welcome to the
most exciting era in the history of mankind. I give to you
the essential knowledge that you will need to transcend

worry, lack, suffering and boredom, in order to witness, experience and embody nothing but exuberance, love, beauty and inspiration.

You have been taught and trained backwards. You were taught to view authority as coming from outside yourself. You are scared into believing that you will be punished if you don't listen to your elders, your teachers, your government, etc., etc. You will suffer if you do not accept what someone else defines as right and wrong and then act accordingly. Instead of being told to think for yourself and decide what is right and wrong for you, you are to sign over your power to someone else who "knows better". So throughout your life you look to outside sources to define you as good or bad, sick or healthy, productive or lazy. The truth is that if you were to look within to your innate map and compass you would never act outside of the vibrational range of what is true, right and evolutionary. If you were taught to rely on the infinite well of pure wisdom that is always available within you, your quality of life would be exponentially greater than what the majority of the world has come to accept today.

Here is the tough fact that you must swallow if you want to live a life that you enjoy: every event that has ever taken place in your life has been created by infinite intelligence orchestrating the entirety of existence for the sole purpose of your evolution and expansion into greater volumes of joy and unconditional love. For many that is the hardest thing to accept but for all beings it is the most liberating piece of information they could ever hear.

The overall infinite consciousness that orchestrates and materializes all that exists from itself will always produce what is necessary for the evolution and expansion of your specific individuation of awareness. The overall consciousness has made its power fully available to you. But as children we are subject to the manifestations of those around us because we are not able to fully comprehend, claim or wield our potential and power. In our current society we are being conditioned to remain ignorant of our power. Therefore, until you begin to perceive the signs given to you by the higher consciousness in the way that they are intended to be received you will not claim your power and will continue to be subjected to manifestations perpetuated by others outside of you. Many of these people whose manifestations you will have to swallow if you do not step into more of your true potential have been conditioned to be controlling and manipulative or have been conditioned to be fearful and perpetuate miserable circumstances for themselves and many others.

Eventually you will run into those who have discovered and embodied their true potential and power to differing degrees and in different ways. If you listen to your past conditioning you will most likely try to "rationalize" or explain away the truths and realities they perpetuate. But if you listen to your heart or your unsoiled and unadulterated intuition you can begin to accept and explore your power in your own divinely unique way.

From this point of view , as you read this book, when I say you are the Omni powerful creator of your reality and the reality you perceive is a direct reflection of your thoughts feelings and emotions, remember that this is only the case tif you are consciously cultivating your own vibrational state. If you experience a reality that is undesirable, traumatic or mundane it is most likely because you are portioning off your power and assuming that you are not in control of your reality. This will leave you at the disposal of or under the control of malignant thoughts, manifestations and realities perpetuated by other beings who have not realized or embodied their true moral compass or power. So let's continue with this in mind.

Will you accept this power? Every last minute detail of your life will be nothing more than a projection of your consciousness. Your environment and circumstances have no choice but to reflect and materialize what you choose to think about and the corresponding feelings and sensations that you let your thoughts produce in you. You will never experience or witness anything that you have not produced through your consistent vibratory quality and presence. When we hear this our conditioned mind wants to go straight into blaming ourselves for all the undesirable circumstances and events that we have experienced, but I encourage you to ignore that inclination for now. Stay centered here in the present moment and train your focus on the future while I expand your knowledge of the infinite power available to you. I promise that if you can do this, if you can forget about the past for just a little while it will pay off immensely. If you slip into deciphering your past manifestations through a soiled lens you will only waste time and portion off pieces of your power to forces within you that don't deserve any of your time and energy.

The answers that you have been naturally searching for all of your life are far simpler than you would ever assume. This amazing simplicity pervades the infinite complexity that we are coming to understand. I believe that part of the human condition is to over-complicate, over-think, over-analyze and hesitate. In our quest to find our true power we actually hinder and eliminate most of that power by imagining that outside forces have any power over us. When in actuality we are placing every molecule we perceive right where we find it and endowing it with any power that it has. Settling into this realization takes diligence and vigilance. You must remember to paint everything in your life with this brush. When you perceive an outside force that is seemingly exhibiting its own will over you or controlling you in some way remind yourself that you placed that apparition there and you placed it there with a purpose. You chose to place that force there so that you could learn a specific lesson and expand your consciousness in a specific way. If you do not particularly

4

like the apparitions you have placed in your reality you have to bring your attention into what you're expecting to encounter in your life. You need to begin to project and expect to encounter more preferable and supportive forces out there if you want to experience a more conducive life.

DO NOT slip back into perceiving any person, institution or apparition of any kind as having control over you. Stop adhering to the rules that you have accepted in the past. It is the most insufferable tragedy that in most cases is the accepted standard for adulthood and life. It is as if we have married the spear that shall cleave the spirit from our existence. In our genuine form we are radiant and all powerful.

This book is the beginning of your transformation. The journey of embodying more of your true power is never ending. Every day, every moment is another chance to expand your capability further and further!

If you would like to explore the concepts in this book more in depth connect with us on Facebook. Go join the Superhero Academy Facebook group. The Superhero Academy website is currently being built and polished. The Facebook group will be the best way to stay updated on everything we are doing and when the website will be up and running. The Superhero Academy will be a constantly evolving platform where you will find support and guidance that will help you assimilate the knowledge in this book into your life and experiences. I am designing the Superhero Academy to be a very personal and interactive community. Once the website is up you will be able to take in depth courses that address each of the chapters in this book. Each lesson dissects a concept in this book and then gives you some ideas on how to go out and apply it to your life. Also at the end of each lesson you will have the option to send me a message directly with questions, statements, ideas and requests. I am 100% dedicated to being as available to you as you would like me to be. You are not alone on this journey you have started. Your evolution is fully supported by all of existence including myself and all the innovative and revolutionary teachers associated with the Superhero Academy. Don't hesitate. Jump right in. Read through this book and then come join us in the Facebook group so we can work together to bring more of your innate power to the surface and craft your dream reality.

REALITY

You are the infinite, divine, pure, beauty and love that permeates all things. <u>That is what you are.</u> That is what is reading this right now. Consciousness is orchestrating all of existence constantly, through the awareness that is beyond the electrical impulses taking place on the physical plane we call your brain. You are an individualized point of the source from which all of existence originates. As an agent of that source you choose to precipitate into existence the entirety of the physical plane by the act and means of vibration. So when your awareness, or for most (as I spoke about in the introduction), the subconscious mind, conceives a concept it then projects that out into your experience. Take a minute to consider this proven fact of reality; it goes conceive and then perceive not perceive and then conceive. You strengthen these apparitions by amplifying the vibration through feelings. When you realize that you have constant access to this power you can begin to more consciously and intentionally participate in the creation process.

Your physical brain does not yet contain the full capability to calculate and orchestrate the molecular details of how your chosen creations will come about, so don't concern it with that responsibility. Your responsibility as a physical being is simple; focus on, lean into and amplify with every unit of energy that you expend, the specific quality of vibration or feelings that you desire to experience and know that the source from which all things originate, the true you, is organizing your physical experience to reflect that which you are amplifying. This is a beautiful realization. All that you have to do is maintain the vibrational state that you truly desire and once in a while check in with your physical experience to enjoy the reflections and further strengthen and clarify your preferred vibrational state. If when you check in with your physical reality you perceive something negative or in other words not preferable, decide to coat it or perceive it in a positive way and extract whatever expansive insight presents itself. Then assimilate that fresh knowledge and belief into your constantly evolving mental construct and processes.

By dissecting and investigating the physical level of reality down further and further, smaller and smaller quantum physics has confirmed the infallible truths that the wisest beings have been pointing us towards throughout the history of mankind. I encourage you to investigate and study independently what quantum physics has discovered about the nature of reality. As you do this the most important pieces of evidence that quantum physics has discovered lead you seamlessly to the launching point from which you can cross the gap into the power available to you through knowledge of the characteristics the source, awareness, consciousness and the non-physical endow you with. From the very edge of the physical we look out into what you might call oblivion or mystery and the greatest decisions facing our species present themselves; do we turn back to what seems solid? Do we deny our intuition, our power and potential? Do we choose to ignore what scientists and true spiritual guides have been telling us for millennia? Do we let fear get the best of us and settle for bundles of heinous lies taught to us by others who wanted to keep us small, vulnerable and controllable? The edge of the cliff is getting crowded. So many curious wanderers and seekers are peering out into the grand mystery, the great oblivion beyond the physical. As a collective, human beings are tired of feeling limited, powerless and subject to the will of the malignant powers that be. The only way that this inclination is possible is if there is a higher intelligence beyond the realm of the physical that can give us hints that there is more to us than we have been taught to perceive.

I challenge you to embrace the beautiful truth that you the observer not only affect whatever you observe but orchestrate the entirety of what you observe with the intention of accelerating your evolution and expansion.

POTENTIALITY

You are an individualized expression of infinite intelligence. The sooner you accept that the sooner you will embody more of the freedom, potential and power employed by the all-pervasive source that you come from. While gazing out into the unknown or the oblivion that is the non-physical source of all of existence, you feel as though there are answers, there has to be, regardless of what was published or left unexplained in the scientific or spiritual texts you explored. Your intuition, your inner intelligence, tells you that there are answers and truths available to you that simply cannot yet be explained by science or rational thinking. So many of us simply hang up our inquisitive hats and settle into what we "know", or in other words have been taught to believe. We settle into complacency and join the herd to be guided by whatever trusted Shepard resonates with our conditioned belief structures, whether that be the government or the church, guru's, monks and salesmen of all kinds that promise us that our pot of gold is available for just three easy payments of $19.99. But all the while there is an underlying tension that you are free to ignore, or rather try to ignore, but keeps popping up and causing all kinds of turmoil and chaos within the illusory prisons we build in our bodies

10

and minds.

What you CAN do is: get to that edge of scientific discovery and take a look at the wall they seem to have run into. Instead of shrugging your shoulders, turning around and heading back down the slope of limitation, walk up to the veil and poke a hole to look through. When you do you will find infinity. That's it, the answer you've been looking for isn't going to be found in some complicated formula. The answer is that reality is infinite. So what does that mean for you? If you've come to the precipice of scientific discovery you know that everything in existence is 99.999999999999999......% empty space, or at least we think it is empty. Even when you get down to the unimaginably small center that you think is really "solid matter" it turns out that it is just a fluctuation of energy flashing in and out of existence faster than the speed of light. So you sit down and wrap your head around that for a minute: There is no end to existence it just keeps going on and on and anything that has ever existed already exists and nothing can ever be destroyed or created and what we perceive as real or solid is really just a "void" of seemingly empty space with a bunch of pulses of energy and information flashing in and out of existence faster than the eye can see. That is reality, endless possibilities flashing in and out of existence. So what is governing all of these pulses of energy and information? The perplexing answer that we have come to is that it seems to be us! The observer cannot observe without affecting the observed and at the very base of all existence the observer is made up of the very same nothingness or everythingness as the observed.

So here you are at the cliffs edge of scientific discovery with nothing but infinite potential possibilities taking their cue from your consciousness. You cannot stop knowing this once it has broken the threshold and entered your mind. You can deny it and run away from it all you want but the infinite intelligence that is consciousness within you is never going to let you forget that it is you deciding what possibilities flash into existence next. Every time you choose to scratch your nose or run your fingers through your hair you are affecting reality. You are just a big ball of energy vibrating within a certain range of frequencies and so is everything around you. Every thought you think is nothing more than a vibration, a pulse, an electrical surge echoing outward into infinity and manipulating and aligning all other vibrational units of matter in the cosmos to create the illusory image before you that matches your resonance.

Each and every millisecond that you are aware of is an effervescent opportunity to alter the slice of reality that you will see next. One important distinction to always keep in mind is that you are not altering the slice of reality that is directly in front of you in the "now". The slice that is in front of you now was created by your vibrational quality in the past. You are influencing the very next slice of slate, and the next, and the next, and the next. Each and every alteration you decide to make echo's off into infinite possible openings exponentially. But you can jump from one set of exponential infinite possibilities to a completely different location in the sea of the infinite with no effort at all. The most important factor in this equation is your vibration. It is truly the only factor in the equation because your vibrational range comprises the entirety of the reality that you experience in each and every instant. So take the slice of reality you are experiencing right now and freeze it. Divide it down to a millisecond. Now take the time out of it completely. Just one section of reality cut from the block of infinity. In that seemingly finite slice nothing can exist apart from consciousness and awareness in its truest definition (you could rename these as matter if you want to dumb it down but it will serve you to remember that matter is just intelligence or information and energy). Now while you consider this fact also remember that what you can perceive on that particular slice of reality is only one configuration of energy out of an infinite amount of possible configurations that you could be perceiving in that moment. Look at this page in front of you. In reality there is the page where you perceive it and the very same page is pressed up against your eyeball and in between where you perceive the page to be and your eyeball there are an infinite number of pages. This may sound irrational to your conditioned mind that wants to leave it at the simple answer of the page is over there, but this isn't some freaky-deeky, weekend at the music festival shit, this is pure science. Welcome to the age where we not only discover quantum physics but we transcend it and learn who and or what we actually are, what lies beyond the veil of perception and how capable we are when it comes to manipulating reality.

Capability

All boundaries and confines are self-created. What your mind can conceive is truly limitless so when you perceive a barrier or restraint it is your own creation. If the mind can create limits it can dissolve them just as easily. The entirety of the universe and all things in existence are at the mercy of your authority. The fabricated limitations of your ancestors are stored in your DNA but the fact remains that those inherited ceilings are sustained only through your mental adherence to them. The moment you accept your true capability and sever your attachment to a perceived limitation you transcend its existence entirely and you are free to expand your consciousness, actions and endeavors as you desire.

You are capable of anything that your imagination can produce and your imagination also decides how long it will take you to accomplish it or what you will have to do to accomplish it. If anywhere along the way you decide with conviction that you can't do it, then you won't do it. But then, at any time, you can decide again that without a doubt you are going to do it and then it again becomes possible and you decide the means and circumstances that must occur for that goal to become a reality simply by believing a certain way. When you know that something is going to happen and doubt does not ever enter your mind anymore it will simply be. Make a statement and dial your focus down and into the existence of what you state and do not entertain any other image, words or concepts in your head and then it simply will be. When you begin to practice this and doubt or limiting beliefs come up pick them apart piece by piece and shine your new light, of knowing that your power cannot be hindered upon them, until they are consumed by your preferred beliefs and cease to exist to your awareness. The way to do this is to simply hold the exuberant sensation of the end goal already existing in every cell of your body and zoom in on that until nothing else enters your consciousness and then feel the tangible movement and motion of energy bursting forth from every cell in your body and every point of your infinite existence to take form as that desire being fulfilled.

Non-Verbal Thought

It is useful to drop your attachment to verbal thought patterns. They have their place and they are naturally beautiful, but we are limiting our power and experience by adhering so strictly to the verbal labels that we have been taught. We limit a portion of reality to the confines of a word and relate to things only through our verbal interpretations of them. Experience things as they are. Decide to experience all of creation at once for a few seconds and come into the space where you experience larger packets of information at once. Perceive things through a wider lens so to speak. The words come and go but if you tune into the sensation of embracing all of existence as yourself you can **feel** larger amounts of information in one instant than you would have previously thought possible. Verbal thoughts point to and imitate more evolved and efficient ways of interpreting the infinite amount of information in each instant. Words assume, constrict, deafen, dampen and imitate the effervescent, explosive, intoxicating, progressive, evolutionary, transcendental, infinite potential amounts of information that we can possibly interpret, process, integrate and put to positive use.

Words are simply vehicles that we have invented to carry the more ethereal feelings, sensations and ultimately vibratory resonance of concepts and experiences. Since we have invented them we ought to use them to the best of our ability to express ourselves, communicate and understand the world we are creating. But for now it will serve you to transcend the incessant attachment to verbal thought to accelerate your evolution.

Ping-Pong Game Analogy

Envision life as a ping-pong game happening way faster than the speed of light. The ball itself is your attention and perception. At one end of the table is your infinite intelligence, higher self or source. At the other end is your circumstantial or physical self. When the ball reaches the player it becomes that player because you are not just a little ball of awareness being whacked around, you are the players, paddles, ball, table and venue simultaneously. But in this analogy you embody certain roles within the whole at certain times, much like you do in life. So the lower or physical-self lays down a weak serve or in other words a limiting belief. The higher self sees this and blows the play out of the water. Now here is the important part: The higher-self struck your perception with such force because your "serve" or limiting belief was untrue and so the higher self is trying to shock you out of that way of thinking, because the higher self is not going to allow an individual piece of itself that has access to the whole of its infinite power to believe that it is smaller or less powerful than it is. So now as the lower self you have a choice to make. You can either feel bad about your serve and say, "I'm no good at this.", which will cause you to play an even weaker serve for your higher self to reject. Or you can say, "OK, that serve or limiting belief was obviously untrue because my higher-self struck my perception with a very tangible amount of force. Now I have the opportunity to put a more empowered and savvy serve or belief with my own special spin into play." When you do the higher-self echo's back a playable or actionable ball or piece of evidence and as you follow this trail of exciting agreement between you and your higher self the game or your life ensues in a beautiful, synchronized dance or play. <u>The point is that how you choose to perceive the echo's, evidence and sensations coming from your higher self is what determines the outcomes and reality that you experience.</u>

Keep returning with more empowered and more joyful beliefs and actions and you will develop an unbreakable infinite correspondence with your higher self, which makes for a more beautiful, expansive and enjoyable life.

Begin to notice the more subtle underlying meaning behind your resistance to any situation. Recognize that the only reason you experience resistance or negative guttural reactions is because:

A. You do not wish to experience that configuration of reality similar ones in the future.

and or

B. Your higher self is letting you know that you need

to choose to perceive the circumstance in a more empowered, positive way in order to move into more preferable realities in the future.

You will notice that when you feel bad about something and then follow that with more thoughts and feelings that confirm you are not the creator of your reality, you will always feel worse. Therefore if you want to feel good, anytime you encounter something you do not wish to experience and or feel in the future, first state that you <u>deserve </u>a more desirable experience and then accept that the only purpose of your current experience is to refine your ideas about what you wish to experience. Then follow that up with remembering that in order to experience a more preferable reality all you have to do is hold the feelings you will experience when you are in that new reality throughout your entire being more frequently and eventually constantly. Once you have gone through this mental process ask yourself what physical action you can take as soon as possible, preferably immediately, that will get you closer to this objective and or make you feel happier and more free, limitless and powerful.

CHOICE

Begin to see each and every moment as an opportunity, a platform upon which you can build and launch whatever it is that you choose. Let go of the belief that the reality you experience is stand-alone from your influence. We have been trained to react to the circumstances we perceive as if they are separate from us and our only power is to be affected by them. This is backwards. Physical reality is a reflection of your past emotional attitudes and analytic speculations or judgements. The matter that you see in front of you is nothing more than a neutral canvas that you have shaped and molded by means of your feelings, thought patterns and the meaning or worth that you have endowed past appearances with. You must refine your perception of reality. Physical matter is inherently neutral. Manifestations do not have any power or meaning apart from what you endow them with. You can sculpt an object to mean something positive to you or something negative. All of reality stands independent from meaning and influence. Meaning and influence are the life-force that you command and utilize to create the reality that you perceive. So the reality that you are currently perceiving is just a canvas upon which you paint your future reality. If

18

you want to experience your preferred reality you must break the habit of perceiving your reality as separate from your influence. You have created everything that you see in front of you. You are now creating every circumstance that you perceive in your physical reality instead of accepting aimless expressions of redundant reluctance, hostility and enslavement. So if you are experiencing something that you do not enjoy <u>don't judge yourself for creating it</u>. Simply begin to investigate your belief systems and thought patterns that have created that circumstance. You have unlimited power in each and every moment to choose to perceive things in a different way to craft a more preferable physical reality. You are using your power at all times. You cannot diminish your power over the source energy that makes up all of reality. You can give your power away to others but even that is you using your power. When you give your power to external circumstance or outside forces you are simply stating to the universe or your higher self that you do not wish to craft and cultivate what you see. You do not want to be the artist creating the images that you perceive or you do not believe in the miraculous dynamism required for you or anything to exist at all, let alone as a sentient being endowed with such intrinsic awareness and free will. So you agree to perceive whatever the random ideas lodged in your subconscious bring about. **<u>Why would you do this?</u>** If you are the creator of your reality and you wish to experience a different circumstance than all you have to do is choose to imagine and ,more importantly, believe in something else. Stop giving away your power to the random ideas you have collected throughout your life. Those ideas do not belong in your awareness. Infinite intelligence tells you this by sending negative or bad feelings and sensations through your individualized self. Your personality structure is not a static being that you have no power over. Our power is quite simple, we have just developed the habit of seeing it as complicated and believing that making changes is difficult. When you begin to see that making changes is easy your personality or inner space will begin to bloom at a beautiful rate.

Begin to ignore what "the past you" or powerless you, would say or think about what is in front of you and choose a more expanded point of view. Always know that you are observing the reality you create from beyond form, beyond physical reality. At first this may feel like a shock or a surge of energy that explodes from your core and carries you out beyond any current physical form. As you become comfortable in your creator role you begin to see that the physical reality that you are creating and shaping every minute of every day is just another part of your state of being or a precise reflection of your thoughts, feelings and beliefs. Your boundaries, walls and horizons expand to include all of existence past, present and future (because time does not truly exist as we know it, which I will explain further in the next chapter). So from this new point of view you see that you have the power to choose to create anything that you desire. Your creation is not limited to the desires of "others" but you understand and respect their point of view while you honor your own desire and in doing so stretch their boundaries as well. You may begin to question your desires and ask yourself if you really want all the things that you thought you wanted. This is a very good thing. In those moments you are refining your vision and your desires.

You may begin to see that all of creation is neutral and valid and that anything that you decide is worthy of desiring is worthy of precipitating into your physical reality because there cannot be any limitation that you do not believe in. These phases of questioning and refining your desires are beautiful. They allow you to more clearly see what matters and what doesn't. After a session or period of this clarification you begin to really respect your desires.

Today is A Great Day To Manifest The Shit Out Of Some Abundance

You no longer question them as much and as your trepidation is eradicated your power to create is amplified <u>exponentially</u>.

TIME

Think of the classic descriptions of time that you hear often. Time flies, time flies when you're having fun, where did the time go, time seemed to just drag on, the hours flew by, time stood still. For a moment just forget what you know about time. Forget what the physicist's say, forget what your parents taught you, forget what your guru's say, just clear your mind of all the knowledge, ideas and theories you have absorbed about time. Now from a non-biased point of view begin to measure time. You can't count in seconds because that was just something you were taught and even if you wanted to, you never know if you are measuring each second accurately. You can't really place a measurement on time that hasn't been taught to you and when you try you might begin to feel like the amount of "time" that is passing is of no consequence any way. All you really know is the eternal present. Your physical mind awareness only ever fully experiences the present. You might argue that you can recall a memory or imagine the future but you are still doing that in the present and those reflections and images are filtered through your perception of the present as well. So centered in the present you might begin to ask well how many moments have passed since that specific event happened in the present but without referring to your conditioning about time or in other words the ideas you were taught about time, you can't really measure it. It is illusory. Not to say that time does not pass or that it is of no use to us. We simply need to recognize and utilize our influence over that portion of our creation. The measurement of time can be a valuable tool but not until you drop all limiting beliefs about it. I encourage you to begin to develop your own unique, more malleable systems for measuring time. See that you can manipulate your perception of time by giving yourself permission in whatever way makes sense to and stretches your conditioned beliefs about it. This is a very non-physical and unique practice for anyone who dives into it. What works for one may not make sense to another. But simply relax your mind and release your conditioned thoughts and then slip into a new perception free from any constraining beliefs about time or slip into a stream of perception that does not acknowledge the concept of time. From an unattached place you can decide how you would measure the length, width or depth of your experience. I usually choose to measure time only when necessary. I like to drop any ideas about the time and instead measure my experience in terms of excitement and intrigue.

Take your new point of view about time out into your everyday interactions and activities. You will see that you have a ton of preconceived ideas about how much time it should take to complete certain tasks and activities and those ideas heavily influence how much effort you exert and what you think you are capable of. Begin to notice that time is always controlled by you. You can prolong or accelerate your perception of time. This is not done through massive effort, to the contrary it is done by relaxation. If you are really enjoying an appearance in front of you just settle into it. Relax into the details of it. Let your awareness soak it up and you will begin to notice that time slows down and every "second" can last a lot longer and contain much more information than you previously perceived. Likewise, if you must go through a certain task or activity that bores you or makes you feel heavy in any way relax into the realization that you can place your awareness somewhere else or on something else. Lose track of your immediate physical circumstances or the appearances in front of you. In other words, lose yourself in your imagination. See yourself under a waterfall or climbing up a mountain or floating around in thin air. State to yourself that you are going to imagine something that you have never imagined or thought of before and relax as the images pour in. It's not necessary to look for meaning in these images. The meaning and necessary realizations will automatically be downloaded into your consciousness without any effort on your part. Before you know it your number will be called at the DMV or the line at the store will have dissipated.

Once you have experienced your ability to slip out of your current physical circumstance begin using this realm in your mind to envision your pure, true and unhindered desires and endow your physical being with the vibration of that reality to strengthen your power to consciously manifest a more preferable reality.

SPACE

Space is an illusion, Awareness is infinitely Present at all points of and beyond physical existence.

Space is a great concept to dissect as an entrance point to realizing the validity of infinity.

We tend to think of space as a measurement or a measurable void of dense physical form. The concepts and ideas we learn and adopt about space are valid and they are great sign-posts, but that's all they are. As you dissect your preconceived ideas about space, as you go deeper and deeper into the nature of the idea you begin to reach the brink of physical reality. You find the border between form and the formless. Now remember that the air around you is form. Anything on the physical plane is what you would call form. In outer-space or outside of our atmosphere we know space to essentially be a vacuum with bundles of gases and dust, stars and galaxies floating around. But beyond the molecules and atoms that we can perceive through our limited physical senses exists 99.9999999999999999999…% of what we can conceive. Beyond form, even that which we cannot perceive through our physical senses but only conceive in our minds is the concept of limitless potential. Literally all of form flashes in and out of existence originating from an infinite source. You cannot escape this fact. Infinity, beyond all physical representations or concepts, means that everything that our physical minds could ever or have ever conceived exists simultaneously and cannot be subtracted from or added to, cannot be confined or end. So if you throw a rock into a field, envision a rock at every point as far as the eye can see. That is reality, but you as the observer endowed with free will perceives a specific configuration of this physical energy or vibration and you have chosen to perceive different configurations one by one sequentially. You have also decided to make sense of these configurations however you choose and refer to them however you choose and (here is the important part) you decide to perceive the next configuration of source energy as being in relation to another. You precipitate or agree to observe the next configuration in a way that makes sense to the physical constructs you have agreed to endow with your observation or awareness. As awareness you experience nothing outside of free will. You are experiencing all of creation or physical configurations that consist only of your choice or agreement.

Now step back into your physical brain, your human brain and you will find a whole bunch of ideas, concepts, agreements and activity that your emotional guidance system is letting you know through bad feelings that you do not wish to observe at all or in the same way when you move into the next configuration. Now here is concept that trips us up the most when we want to change our experience; you cannot destroy or create any configuration of source energy. You cannot remove it from existence within infinity. You can only agree to perceive a new or different image. From this point of view, it becomes obvious that acknowledging or observing the configuration you have decided you do not prefer is the only reason it is "visible" or perceived by your awareness. Through the constructs you have decided to use to observe other configurations of yourself, it is accepted that time or space can occur and so you perceive that certain configurations must follow or precede others in order to make sense of, or relate one image to the other. But from this point of view you begin to decide or discover that the nature in which one configuration relates to, or in other words effects the next, is malleable and ultimately under the influence of your free will.

This is the magic, the holy grail. I know it seems too simple to be so but you will not find more power than this in any degree of complexity. How one slice of reality effects the next slice is up to you and the thoughts and emotions you decide to conjure up about that slice.

The substratum or closest to nonphysical construct of physical reality your human brain can perceive as of yet is vibration. So far that is as deep or as small as we have been able to discover or make sense of. Vibration is the underlying substance of all of the physical world that we perceive. So if you want to begin to more consciously choose the images that you will perceive next you must start with vibration. Start with the vibration that you are sending out from this individualized physical mind/body configuration that you have endowed with observation or awareness.

IMAGINATION

The truth is always ringing. It's that underlying tone that you cannot shake. Thoughts and emotions scrape the surface and cause disruptions, distortions, ripples. But in your core is the eternal chord of reality. The elegance of the limitless power of the nonphysical source is engrained in each of the trillions of cells that compose this shell you inhabit. So in truth you are an immutable source of pure light, vivacity and brilliance. All of our human experiences wash away. They only exist as long as you give them your attention. Each instant, every second is a fresh slate. We attach ourselves to our previously conditioned thought processes so tirelessly that we lose touch with the infallible power that is inherent within us. I don't mean to disregard or diminish the palpability of our emotions, they matter, they direct us. But the truth is that your life will blossom into exactly what you prefer it to be and much more when you decide to choose the emotions and continuously emit the vibration that feels good. Keep moving your awareness and imagination forward, perpetually onto more shockingly wonderful visions and experiences.

The End of Questions as We Know Them

When you begin to see questions as an opportunity instead of a lack of knowledge it is an amazing feeling. If you can ask the question the answer is within your consciousness as well. 99% of the time we only ask questions because we don't trust that the answer our higher self presents is true, or we are not tuned into our innate intelligence enough to see the truest answer and so we entertain many answers and look to "outside" sources for input. The amount of questions you have is a direct reflection of how much of your power you are willing to give away. So when you embrace your power more and more naturally any question that comes up comes with the simplest and purest answer attached and ringing clear. Trust that the divine in you cannot lead you astray. The answer is your preference. What do you prefer the answer to be? That can be the answer if you allow it to be or more importantly if you believe it to be. Do not give weight, thought or observation to other people's answers unless they resonate with your preference or expand the volume of love and light that your preference is capable of containing.

My point is not that you should stop asking questions all together. My point is to inspire you to see questions in a whole new way. See the act of asking as an opportunity and desire to connect with the infinite intelligence available to you at all times and receive guidance as to what you truly desire and prefer and how to most efficiently bring that into existence.

If you take just one moment to allow the divine intelligence within you to guide your step you will find the next worthy adventure with effortless ease. Even after conquering the most formidable mountains your mind may stir with thoughts of limitation and trepidation. But the channel of energy running adjacent to those fear based thoughts is pure and untainted guidance from a realm that you are beginning to create, tune into and realize. It is easier to slip into the flow of limitless potential and innate love than it is to dwell in the stagnant waters of fear and self-doubt.

So what is the most inspiring and exiting thing, situation or circumstance that you can imagine right now. Close your eyes and paint the most overwhelmingly beautiful and magical scene that you can possibly conceive. As you settle into that vision keep expanding it to embody more wonder, vitality and excitement. Notice the details with as much clarity and passion as you can. Now notice the specific and divine feelings, sensations and vibratory qualities that this vision produces in you and decide to carry that with you at all times. Coat everything you see with that tone, that effervescent clarity and expansive state of passion.

Keep returning to your infinite imagination to produce and refine new, more beautiful and celestial visions at all times. Never stop crafting your reality from this limitless realm that is always available to you.

CONVICTION

The only way to give more gifts to yourself and humanity is by being as vibrantly yourself as you can at all times. You are undeniably original. There is not a single other person who has ever lived, is living or will ever live that can be just like you. You have the privilege of being whatever and whoever you choose to be in each and every moment and it is all yours.

A good place to start shining brighter is by giving material or monetary gifts but do it with the proper vibratory attitude of knowing that your source is infinite and flowing freely. Give bigger tips, give money to homeless people, bring presents anywhere you go. Get creative. Give gifts in a way that has never been done before or is rarely done. Do this with a joyful demeanor because you know that you will always have more than you could ever imagine flowing too and through you faster than the speed of light and you enjoy making any persons' experience more exciting and enjoyable.

Start smiling and being more energetic, gentle and excited in your everyday interactions. The interactions that you used to perceive as mundane or draining suddenly become charged with divine energy and opportunities to have a noticeable impact on your experience. These gifts of radiant interaction alter the fabric of your world beyond what you can do with physical or monetary gifts alone because they employ the most powerful energy of unconditional love and compassion in motion. Enter every interaction with another human being coming from an invincible place of generosity, especially generosity of your animated personality and playful demeanor. See each and every person out there in the world as a light being. What I mean is see them as a bundle of light and energy. See them as the creator of their own world and a blissful addition to yours, placed there by your vibratory resonance.

Transcending Fear of Judgment

Be willing to let more of your true self out into the world. Many people are squeezing themselves into molds that they do not belong in because somewhere along the line somebody told them that they should. You have to get excited about blazing your own trail. There is an infinite well of creativity and splendor teeming within you and as soon as you open the floodgates it will overwhelm your world and create your ultimate nirvana right before your eyes. The only thing that can limit the blissful flow of your creation is your own mind. For most people inspiration strikes and then is doused with thoughts of limitation and doubt, but if we would stop pissing all over our inspired ideas our lives and our world would be entirely different. Be willing to go out into the world and be yourself. Stop caring what other people will think of you. 99% of the time they are not thinking about you at all and if they are they are wondering what you think of them. So when it comes to the .5% of the time when somebody actually does judge you or thinks something negative about you, who cares! It does not pose any literal threat to you. You can waste your entire life playing it safe due to fear of judgement. Even if everyone in the world judged you it would not do you any harm whatsoever. If you are not a judgmental person you will not attract judgmental people into your life and if they do appear you won't notice because your thoughts are centered in the abundance of value that you can gain from that interaction. So drop the unnecessary worries about whether you will be liked or whether you will be safe. The more you strive to be yourself and shine your infinite light upon the world the more you will be liked. As you embody a more genuine personality and demeanor people will be naturally drawn to you. You become a magnet for positive reinforcement and support.

Conditioning

When we are young, before others have filled our heads with their opinions, laws, facts, etc. etc. we can feel the source of infinite knowledge and wisdom as inseparable from ourselves and every configuration that we experience. We don't put it into words and phrases because we don't need to, but we feel it emanating from our core naturally. Some of the people in our lives actually pass on knowledge and opinions that help us to discover and embody more of our power but along the way many concepts take root in our minds that lead to doubt, fear, anger and sadness and those are all false ideas. The very nature of what you are does not allow for any fear or doubt, anger or sadness. You are nothing but infinite power. Your awareness is truly infinite. The only way you can experience negative emotions is if you believe in the possibility of harm or deprivation coming to you. People tell us that in order to avoid harm and deprivation we can't do x, y or z and we most certainly must dedicate our lives to bullshit that sucks the joyous life right out of our veins. But when you see that you are the intangible, non-physical awareness that animates all things in existence, the infinite source beyond your physical body, you realize that whatever happens to your physical self cannot touch your true self and was actually created and manifested by entertaining belief in whatever "negative" appearance presented itself to your physical self.

In order to expand your consciousness and embody more of your innate power it will sometimes be necessary to encounter our conditioned beliefs, investigate these apparitions, their roots and origins and then make the decision to dissolve their influence over us and their existence within our awareness. Do not place to much weight and complication on this process. Decide to use whatever methods seem easy and light to you in your efforts to dissolve limiting beliefs and replace them with empowered thought processes and belief structures.

In this chapter I have presented you with just a few examples of methods that have helped me to restructure my mental activity. I assure you that the quickest and most efficient ways of doing this is to relax into it, discover and craft whatever practices or methods feel easiest and most accessible to you. Let ideas come and go and see that they are just apparitions that you are creating. They do not have any power over you that you do not give them. If you want to experience joy, love, passion, exuberance and creativity focus on those things and the feeling states that they produce. It really is that simple. Dissolve all suffering through acting on and adhering strictly to ideas and belief systems that make you feel good.

Constantly expand the horizons and volume of joy that your being experiences and in turn emits by repetitively asserting your preferred vibratory state. This will set you free!

Labeling

An extremely important practice to adopt in your quest to create your dream reality is to begin to label every appearance as working to bring you your highest good.

First and foremost, every appearance that you see is a message or gift from your higher self that is specifically designed to bring you more joy. Many of us have developed the habit of labeling appearances we don't prefer as negative. But what we fail to realize is that anytime we label anything as negative we are distancing ourselves from our highest good and dream reality by overlooking the valuable nuggets and expansive insights the circumstances contain. When you encounter an appearance that is not preferable start by labeling it as a gift or message from your higher-self right away and you will instantly sense a realization that expands your consciousness.

For example, let's say you encounter an angry person. Instead of reacting in an angry way and allowing their vibration to infect your being, start by realizing that this is an opportunity to expand your consciousness. Then you will be inspired to investigate what parts of yourself this person is reflecting; since everything you see in the physical world is a direct reflection of something you have entertained in your awareness. So then you will realize instantaneously that you have reacted out of anger in the past and instead of judging yourself for those past experiences thank your higher self for showing you this and decide to eliminate the part of yourself that has the capacity to act in this non-preferable way. Then in the future when you encounter a situation that would have previously inspired anger you will feel relief from that and instead embrace a state of non-resistance and peaceful resolution or whatever else may be required to transcend the non-preferable appearance all together.

Journal Entry

Write a journal entry from the point of view that you will have when your dream life has become manifest. Use this exercise to cultivate the tangible sensations that you want to experience. The source does not speak, or listen to words as much as it listens to the vibratory state that you are emitting in conjunction with the words. So it's not the verbal or linguistic thoughts that you think over and over so much as the movement of energy that those words, stories and ideas produce and maintain. You most likely have heard this before, your affirmations won't bring about the results that you're looking for if while you're practicing the affirmation you are allowing a doubtful feeling to exist within you. So remove yourself from your current reality, circumstances, conditioning, thoughts and ideas. Become completely still and simply acknowledge that you are all that is. Your awareness is present in equal and infinite volume at every point of existence and from that state delve into your dream life and begin producing the images sensations and thoughts that you will have when your life is exactly how you would set it up if there were no such thing as limitations. Now as you open your eyes and begin to write this journal entry settle into the realization that there are no limitations. The only limitations that you will experience are those that you agree to perceive.

Say to Yourself:

Everything that exists,
Everything that has ever existed,
Everything that will ever exist,
Every thought that has ever been entertained,
Every action that has ever been taken,
Every single fluctuation of energy and information that has ever taken place
supports me in this moment and is constantly showing me my highest good.
Nothing can ever create distance between me and the most profound and beautiful experiences that I can

36

imagine.

Every experience that I have is fully intended for the sole purpose of my expansion and joy.

I now choose in every instant to join the entirety of existence, including the infinite non-physical realm,

in embracing my full power and creating more abundance,

more joy,

more love,

more creativity,

and more exuberant vitality

than I can even begin to imagine from this point of view.

I relinquish my obsession with the how, when, what, where questions

and allow my divine soul to blissfully and creatively orchestrate my path and my journey so that I can fully enjoy more of the celestial sensation I choose to experience.

I know that as I dive more willingly into the recognition and experience of this amazing sensation

I am allowing more and more beauty, love, wisdom and celebration to come to me.

I declare that each instant is an endless well of pure excitement, peace and happiness.

Vigilance

Setting your intention is the joy of life. Discovering and uncovering exciting ideas and opening up fresh and new realms of your imagination is where you will find the most joy. The realization and manifestation of these ideas and desires is wonderful and will be integral to your expansion. But it is all too often that people get lost in the appearances themselves. You assume that your joy is directly connected to the material forms that you desire when in actuality the bliss, excitement, passion and ultimate happiness is in the expansion and experience that the appearances produce and inspire in your awareness. So you must adopt vigilance and constantly remind yourself to not get attached to the appearances that you create and produce. Attach yourself to the continual acceleration and expansion of your consciousness, imagination and embodiment of more of your true power. When you manifest something brilliant and exciting feel free to get down into it. Witness and appreciate it in all of its luster and elegance. But when inspiration strikes and you are pulled back into the vortex of your imagination be excited and willing to move along to your next creation. Your creatorship is eternal, unbounded, continual and ever effervescent. Realize that any situation, object, circumstance or manifestation is finite and cannot contain the infinity of your consciousness, joy and imaginative inspiration.

PRACTICAL APPLICATION

As you embrace your true being, the infinitely powerful orchestrating consciousness, you see that physical reality is an illusion, a reflection of you and your vibratory state. All of the smoke and mirrors around you are, at the very base level, powerless over you. Remember that meaning and significance are the life-force employed and assigned by you. You will notice that when you are not dynamically choosing your thoughts and feelings in order to cultivate your preferred vibratory resonance within, things may seem meaningless because now you know that the only way anything has any meaning at all is because you decide it does. So here is where it may get a little tricky. There are people and events going on in your reality that are beyond a shadow of a doubt negative, scary, evil or whatever else you may be calling it. But remember that any part of your physical reality is there to remind you and motivate you to expand, grow, refine and embrace more of the infinite potential that is always available to you. In order to transition into a consciousness that is more aligned with your higher self you will have to change your beliefs, patterns, routines and behavior. You will not be able to sustain a higher vibratory state if you do not choose to alter the segments of your physical reality that have kept you imprisoned in a less preferable, lower

39

vibratory state. Ultimately the only practices and activities that will destroy the walls you have built around yourself are the ones that feel best to you. No other person can be the ultimate authority, they can only point you in the right direction and give you helpful suggestions that you will perceive and act upon in your chosen way. When you encounter a negative circumstance or configuration of physical reality do not dwell on it or make it a permanent fixture in your reality. Take any negative circumstance as a message from your higher self to eradicate the portions of your vibratory state that allow manifestations of a lower vibratory quality to exist.

Cut through all the self-propagated bullshit going on in your head. You don't have to tolerate anything. Simply paint over whatever it may be that your "tolerating" with a more inspired vibrational frequency. Do this now! Choose to broadcast or emit a more powerful vibration at all times, always building on itself and outshining the previous state you cultivated within. It's a choice, it's a choice, it's a choice, it's a choice, choice, choice, choice, Choose! Choose clarity, single mindedness, purpose, vision, confidence, assuredness, the flow. Stop dipping toes and forget about the shore all together. Don't hold back. Be bold, be out there, go for it! Why shouldn't you? Stop asking yourself for permission and start making statements. Just make a decision! What are you 110% pumped about right now? If it's truly all up to you, and it is, why do you need to stall or hinder or wait? Just relax into your power, your innate ability.

Find what feels good to you. There are endless ways to tune into your higher self's inspiration. Pick the ones that are immediately available to you. Trust that your desires are valid and stop feeling bad about feeling good. Our society has amplified the strange paradigm that if you do what excites you or what feels good to you, you are somehow bad or irresponsible. This is not the case. When you embrace your own moral compass, when you begin to define right and wrong through trusting your heart and you higher self's guidance. You will not infringe upon anyone else's happiness or jeopardize your integrity because you acknowledge that reality is infinite and you do not have to remove anything from someone else's reality to conjure something into your own.

You should honor the historical data and teachings that resonate for you. Many creators have found and refined processes and practices that will aid you in your mission to transcend your current reality and create a more pristine and dynamically beautiful reflection. So start by learning about and experimenting with the activities that are calling out to you but that your lower, fear based, mind is afraid to encounter. Examples of these would include yoga, exercise, being in nature, travel, drinking more water, consuming less toxins, soaking up the sun, meditation, conversing with other people who are in a similar vibratory state as you. These are some of the basic practices that will give your vibration a huge boost. You should also begin to craft your dream reality in your head without limitations, as I talked about in the chapter on imagination, and notice when your physical reality starts to change and shift due to your shift in consciousness. When things begin to show up or drop out of your reality go ahead and investigate them and celebrate where you are doing a great job of maintaining your chosen vibratory state and also take stock of the parts that still need refining and celebrate those realizations as well.

Some of the off the beaten path practices that I have enjoyed experimenting with are listed below. Feel free to give them a try, alter them, or ignore them as feels appropriate to you. But always keep in mind that these are just sign posts and suggestions that I have put here to encourage you to go forth and experiment with until you are able to decide what is perfect for you.

Find a small and simple physical object that holds meaning for you. I choose translucent stones, mainly quartz because, in my reality, quartz has the ability to retain and reflect massive amounts of information and energy. Once you have chosen an object and decided what ethereal qualities it employs in your reality you need to find a way to "charge" it. The purpose of this is to endow it with more of its inherent power and significance. For instance, I have set quartz on a window-sill with the window open for a few nights making sure it gets plenty of sunlight and moonlight. I have also tied quartz to wind-chimes and allowed the beautiful vibratory qualities that the wind chimes produce through sound to expand the talismans horizons. I have held objects in my hand and fed them energy from my body. I have carried objects in my pocket or in a pouch for days, weeks, months, even years. Try some things out and see what method inspires a tangible shift for you when you think of or hold the object of focus. Once you have charged the object sit with it in front of you or in your hand and give your lower mind, ego and fear based thoughts away. Settle into a more relaxed and expansive state of awareness and consciousness. Do this for as long as you want. I usually do it for anywhere between 10 to 30 seconds. From that state non-verbally feel into the sensation of receiving knowledge or information packets from higher self and just allow whatever comes to come. Embrace and enjoy these packages of information and feel into the sensation of allowing them to flow through your awareness and into the talisman that you have chosen and charged. You can feel into the flow of infinite intelligence at any time but this practice is about storing some of these packages of information from higher self in your talisman so that you can come back to that talisman later and experience the information again from a new point of view. Say you have a long hard day of societal obligations and you are feeling drained. Pick up your talisman and allow the information to again course through your awareness and pay specific attention to the tangible sensations of expansiveness and access to the infinite intelligence.

If you believe in synchronicity you will surely begin to see it abundantly in your reality. What we have come to call synchronicity could also be defined as blissful surprises from higher self, thrown right in your face, that reflect a certain vibratory state that you have been cultivating. So use this as a conduit and feed into it. For me the numbers 3, 6 and 9 hold significance because they were mentioned in the first messages I received about synchronicity. So just about anytime I look at the clock the numbers either contain a noticeable arrangement of 3's 6's or 9's or can be added up and divided down to three. So when I started to see 3, 6 and 9 popping up literally everywhere in my reality (because I was looking for it) I started to wonder what it meant. I was hoping that the appearances themselves would show me but I discovered that most of the time I had to define meaning first and foremost. So I started to perceive 3, 6 and 9 as a sign that inspired ideas and expansions in my vibratory capacity were happening then and there and it became my experience. Now when I see multiples of 3 I instantly feel multitudes of new information packets downloading themselves into my awareness. But this is an overly simple representation of synchronicity. Start with this: decide that your higher self is going to give you a noticeable sign, idea or message from someone that will be positive and expansive. Be open to it, don't search for it obsessively just remember that its coming and you don't have to do anything to make it happen. I'll leave it there so I do not mix up my vibratory synchronicities with what your higher self would like to experience through your awareness.

Experiment with sleep cycles. If you are someone who sleeps a lot try staying up all night to watch the sunrise. Or if you are someone who doesn't sleep well at all arrange your circumstances so that you have permission to sleep for 12 hours and go out and exhaust yourself through some crazy physical exercise. Reward yourself with an activity you enjoy afterwards and go to bed with the intention of not waking up until your body has fully recuperated and or downloaded a mass of information that you would like to assimilate into your awareness. You can always play with your intentions before bed and as you wake up. You should do this every time you sleep. Never go to bed without first reflecting on what you would like higher self to endow your personalized awareness with while you are sleeping. Then upon waking reflect on what your intention was before bed and ,without measuring results or trying to decipher what came or didn't seem to come while you were sleeping, instantly define how you intend to feel throughout your waking hours. You don't need words for this, especially since you are coming out of the non-physical awareness or sleep. Simply cultivate and amplify the specific vibratory state and amalgam of sensations that you want to feel for the entire day and just keep doing that for as long as you can. With repetition you will begin to have entire days where you only seldom slipped from your chosen vibratory state. Even if you can only commit to some or all of these practices, concerning sleep, for a couple of minutes or an hour or two you will see your physical reality begin to reflect that conscious decision of altered vibration.

The ultimate key to applying the information in this book and that you are receiving from your higher self is to get off the fuckin couch and go do something that makes you feel good. At the very least sit in a different chair while you meditate. Disrupt your routines and patterns as much as possible. Experimentation with the powerful positive activities and practices that are popping up in your awareness right now are the best way to get out of your old mind and into the paradigm of being a conduit for the flow of infinite intelligence. Find joy in the search, the questions, the experimentation and the expansion of your consciousness because that is the point of life. Move into the flow of infinite intelligence, potential and power by releasing your attachment to the physical reality you have created and shifting your focus to the magic and beauty you are creating in your future.

Experiment with the mysterious and magical practices you feel drawn towards. Follow the ethereal thread of joy and excitement that leads you to and into those magical practices. Push your limits. When you exercise and you feel that rewarding buzz, follow the joyous ideas that come from that state. Let it lead you to your next experiment. When you meditate and you are observing your thoughts find the ones that excite you and make you happy and dive into that stream, that flow. Don't be so concerned with quieting your mind. Be more concerned with feverously following the trains of thought that expand your capacity to embrace joy, happiness, excitement, passion, bliss, intuition and synchronicity. Release ,more and more, the ideas you have adopted from others about what is right and wrong and begin to craft your own moral code. Allow the celestial song emanating from your core at all times to pierce the surface and fill your reality with its unique resonance.

Accept that all practices once only existed in someone's imagination. Create an amalgam of all or some of the practices that make you feel good. Get away from seemingly solid structures and ideas and go into nature and witness the flow, the fluidness, the beautiful resonance of coexistent non-resistance. Become more like that. Embody the qualities you enjoy witnessing. Start with the practices that are obvious to adopt if you want to feel good. These starting points or entrances into the flow have often been pointed to by wise humans for millennia. Yoga, meditation, alchemy and self-alchemy, exercise, travel, reading, writing, adventure, connection, serving others, enjoying nature, creating, inventing, etc. etc. These are the obvious doors into your higher self. Have faith in the inclinations that you have to lean into these. Enter these practices , these streams of divine flow with a whole heart, open mind and with the intention of allowing them to open more doorways of creative expression, blissful realization and passionate living.

So long as it makes you feel powerful it is valuable. Anytime you feel weak in any way you are fooling yourself, you are simply not using your power. Your power is infinite, limitless, celestial. You are the animating awareness. Subtract your awareness from something and it ceases to exist. So spend more time involved in the things that fill you up, that make you so vibrant that your entire being is buzzing. You can trigger this feeling with some deep focused breaths, you can turn on a good song. Start humming, choose to put a skip in your step, no matter what situation or reality you encounter. Start by honoring the sign posts, no matter how small or quiet they are, that you are constantly giving yourself. Trust your gut, your heart and your mind. Infinite intelligence never ever stops giving you suggestions. As you step away from the zombie state and into the knowledge that you are the creator and the chooser, the accelerated and amplified energy that the earth has now moved into position to receive will transform your circumstances with blinding speed. We are no longer in a dense physical world. We have entered a cosmic neighborhood that is more and more non-physical and malleable. Feel into your constant ability and opportunity to transmute and precipitate source energy into whatever vibratory state is truly exciting to you. You are no longer bound to the old rules of the game. You are now the all-powerful conductor of the blossoming symphony orchestra that is your life.

CONCLUSION

Never lose sight of the continual ascension that is always possible. Every configuration of source energy is meant to take you higher. I know from experience that it's easy to travel horizontally and for those who are accustomed to or inspired by ascension it is grueling, it is torture. Your soul has got you by the hair and is begging and pleading for you to rise but for whatever reason you convince yourself that it is ok to remain stagnant. Some sit down on the staircase and concern themselves with the menial dust that has settled there but it's never too late to stand back up and continue your climb. Time and space are creations of man that are used to measure and analyze things and experiences. All that truly exists is RIGHT NOW. What one person chooses not to accomplish in a lifetime you can choose to accomplish today. It's all inside of you. If you immerse yourself in the ascent you will not perceive the length of the journey. All you will know is the

BILL NEWELL

joy that permeates your entire being.

In that moment, that fascinating moment, when your brain sends the message to turn your lips upwards and even if it's just for an instant, you feel that uncontainable, unadulterated exultation swelling from the nethermost particle, overwhelming each cell in your frame and erupting out into the macrocosm. That is the objective that the divine seeks to perform as it invests incomprehensible volumes of impeccable exuberance into each and every electrical impulse taking place within and throughout you. The boundless origin of all of existence has no door, no gate, no off switch. It's always open, all that's required of you is the decision to reach in, grasp a handful of your desire and preference and spread it about as you so please.

About the Author

Bill Newell is a forward thinker. He has been researching spirituality and all the different facets of what could be called "new age" thought for around a decade. He has developed the exceptional habit of distilling all that he finds in his research and writing it down. A conversation with Bill is always an exciting opportunity to learn and discuss the most pressing and exciting questions that are currently facing mankind. Now that he is settled into his role as a leader in this new era of human potential we can expect to see more and more revolutionary content flowing from him. Stay tuned folks, this is an exciting ride and Bill Newell will not leave you hanging.

www.ingramcontent.com/pod-product-compliance
Lightning Source LLC
Chambersburg PA
CBHW061042110426
42740CB00050B/2870